To Maggie Wherever You've Gone

Poems by

Christine Andersen

Winner
of the
2025
Jonathan Holden Poetry Chapbook Contest

Copyright by Christine Andersen 2025

Choeofpleirn Press, LLC

All rights reserved.
This book may not be reproduced, in whole or in part, including illustrations, in any form for any purposes other than scholarly discussion or reviewing, without written permission from the publishers.

Although the author and publisher have made every effort to ensure that the information in this book was correct at press time, the author and publisher do not assume and hereby disclaim any liability to any party for any loss, damage, or disruption caused by errors or omissions, whether such errors or omissions result from negligence, accident,
or any other cause.

Without in any way limiting the author's and publisher's exclusive rights under copyright, any use of this publication to "train" or develop generative artificial intelligence (AI) technologies is expressly prohibited. The author and publisher reserve all rights to license uses of this work for
generative AI training and development
of machine learning language models.

ISBN: (print) 979-8-9991034-0-6
        (digital) 979-8-9991034-1-3

Cover Image by Karen Zimmer

These exquisitely written poems tell a story of trauma, loss and the aftermath with compassion, keen insights and vivid details. As Andersen warns in the first poem, "nature wreaks havoc unexpectedly." Her poems escort us through unexpected havoc, rewarding us with a rich experience while reading Maggie's story.

Sarah Karstaedt, poet

Christine Andersen speaks to the fraught life journey of one person, but the poems relate to all of us as we've "trembled in our own dark hour on the cliff." A powerful, evocative and lovely collection.

David Garnes, author of
Waitin' for the Train to Come In:
A Novel of World War II

Christine Andersen has mastered all the tools and techniques needed to craft fine poems, from line and stanza breaks to alliteration and evocative images. But she creates great poems, which require extraordinary sensibilities, as well. Christine brings depth, richness and nuance to her work. *To Maggie Wherever You've Gone* is a story of tragedy, sadness and confusion – but also understanding, clarity and hope. By reading it, you will have received a very special gift.

Marsha Howland, poet, editor,
co-author of *Practical Writing*.

Contents

Microburst	1
Silent Spaces	2
Country Fashionista	3
Thin Air	4
Photographer's Model	5
Snapshots from the Family Album	6
The Birthday Present	9
Hospital, Hospital	10
Maggie Running	12
The Therapy Room	13
Halloween	14
To Maggie Wherever You've Gone	16
Wind	19
Memorial	20
Things You Left	21
Your Art	23
Loud	24
Blame	25
The Break-Up	26
The Weight of You	28
Unraveling	30
In the midst of heartache—	32
Poem for Your 24th Birthday	33
First Anniversary 2012	34
The Letter	35
Nude Model	37
One Thousand Emails	38
Poem for Your 25th Birthday	40
Ashes to Ashes	41
Scarf	42
How Many Times More—	43
Grief	44

Hemlock	45
Bouquet	46
Second Anniversary 2013	47
Microburst II	48
Acknowledgements	49
About the Author	51
Judge's Comments	53

Microburst

The air sinks in a column,
wind fingers diverge
and upend a swath of stately pines
like matchsticks
dropped from their cardboard box.

Your dad and I encounter the ruin
as we descend the slope
of a familiar trail
in awe of how many trees
went down

overcome with that helpless feeling
when nature wreaks havoc
unexpectedly.
Your dad reaches

for my hand
as we circle and climb
our way through the rubble,
not suspecting
the next disaster

will hit closer to home.

Silent Spaces

Because I'm middle-aged, divorced
and easily flattered by romantic attention,
I buy a big house with my inheritance.
Your dad sells his and moves in,
you and your brother in tow.
You are troubled,
and I feel troubled about you,
a version of a younger me.
I'm haunted
by my own pain with yours so obvious.

You can't hold a job or stay in school
and argue with me about household chores,
run up bills you can't pay.
With tempers ignited, you move and come back.
And sleep until afternoon.

I tell your dad I'm frightened,
but he doesn't want to talk about you.
About us.

I don't press.

From then on,
you brood in the silent spaces
while munitions stockpile behind our eyes
drumming for war.

Country Fashionista

Skinny
as a slinky
silver necklace,
mood rings eclipsing
bony pointer fingers,

You snake into low-rise jeans
size 0,
one bounce for the zip-up
off rose-tinted toes,
your loose tee,
cinched at the waist
by a dog chain.

A curled bob and feather earrings
hiccup off your slender shoulders
as you catwalk to the road
in high metallic heels,
scribbling down the driveway
like pencils on a notebook.

Maggie, small town girl,
you lean against our country mailbox
in slant, late-afternoon light
leafing through
a rag-trade monthly
shopping for identity.

Thin Air

You're a scarf of yourself
a veil
winnowing down
to a whisper.

Your father questions—
have you eaten
don't you need more than that
why such a sour face
did something happen at work?

The doctor delivers the lecture—
you must measure your food
3 ounces of this
5 ounces of that
write it all down
in a notebook—
do you honestly believe that you're eating enough?

Keeping the stethoscope
close to his belly,
he leans in
to hear your reply—

you're soulful
and silent,
sitting cross-legged
on the table,
knees at sharp angles,

fading
like a sigh
into thin air.

Photographer's Model

Off to the city—
waif,
fragile pretzel
with a Gucci bag
filled with lipsticks
for a change of faces

to be a model
potato chip thin,
ribbon candy in the bull's eye
of a photographer's lens,
silk eyes, hollowed cheeks
lashes thick as Japanese fans.

After skimping on a breakfast
downtown,
you smile demurely
as they deep freeze
your innocence
on the glossy page
of a fashion ad—

waif,
sugar wafer,
crumbling
in the box,
rattling your pearls
like round bones.

Snapshots from the Family Album

I.
Eight years old.
You court the grown men
at the party—
jump from lap to lap—
a nymph-like Lolita
while Mommy and Daddy
watch, but don't see.

II.
Twelve years old.
The school counselor refers you
to a psychiatrist who suggests
medication for your depression
after a 15-minute interview.
Your parents, who love you
more than a pill-pushing stranger,
will not drug you.

III.
Sixteen.
A two-week suspension
for filling a thermos
with vodka and passing it around
the school bus.

IV.
Seventeen.
In the dead of winter,

you dress in a blouse and short skirt,
wait for the bus
at the end of the driveway,
refuse to wear a coat to school.
When you complain at night
that you still cannot get warm, your dad
silently applauds the power
of natural consequences.

V.
Eighteen.
A freshman in college.
You sleep with men for drugs
and write the stories in your diary.
You're committed to a hospital
for three days when you tell a girlfriend
you've attempted suicide, but tell your parents
the friend misunderstood.
They believe you. The truth is hidden
in the notebook you keep safely
inside a powder pink pillowcase—
a notebook we didn't find until after—
I pulled my head out of the plastic bag
because I lost my nerve.

VI.
Twenty.
You don't really like the old dog,
even though you grew up with her,
but the money your dad pays
for pet sitting is good.
You don't think the mutt will
run away during the 4th of July fireworks

while you travel to an all-night party
at the beach. We find her
at the pound. You giggle all the way
home, the dog's long, black tail swishing
the backseat, while you repeat,
We sprung her out of jail, we did,
we sprung her out of jail! We—

I'm glad you don't know
your father smothered that old dog
with his bare hand in the garage
a year later—
a mercy killing, he said.
And I suspect the poor dog
was too heartbroken to scream.

The Birthday Present

For your 21st birthday,
your dad buys you a car.
You asked for a shiny one
and he delivers—a BMW, green, 2006,
with heated seats.
Your part:
Paying the taxes, emissions, insurance, registration.
Checking the oil instead of running it empty.

Your trunk grows full of mail
you won't open
dating back two tax years—
bills you refuse to pay because
responsibility would cut the cash flow
from shoes and perfume and bar tabs—

traffic tickets and warnings from the DMV,
insurance premiums, urgent late notices,
medical collection threats—
a mound of paper consequences
for your indifference.

You turn the driver's side door
into a mosaic of cigarette burns
as though it were an ashtray.
The odometer is up 8,000 miles in one spring and
summer.
Eight thousand miles.

Driving the interstates alone,
do you cry or just stare into the hollow nights
resigning yourself to be lost?

Hospital, Hospital

I get the phone call at 2 a.m.
because your dad is away.

Can you pick me up—
I tried to hang myself in the closet
with a scarf—I almost
passed out, but—

When I drive up,
you are sitting outside on the stoop
next to your housemate.

You are quiet in the car,
a pink and white scarf wrapped loosely
about your neck,
crawl right into bed
in a room down the hall from mine
when we get home.

I drive you to your mother's in the morning.

The next time I hear your voice,
it's small.
You're in a hospital somewhere
in rural Massachusetts—
the only place that has a bed.
Someone named Muriel is swearing
in the background while you
cradle the phone at the nurse's desk.
Muriel wants to go home
but you, nonplussed, say
she just needs her medication—

then tell me you avoid
the TV cop shows in the lounge,
read books off the library shelf
in your room instead.

I feel helpless.
They won't let you go outside, and you're a runner.
You wish they had herbal tea.
You pass on group therapy.

Are you talking to anyone, Maggie?
Will you let them help you?

When you get out, you tell me
in the kitchen while we're cooking
that the psychiatrist diagnosed you
with Borderline Personality Disorder and
dissociation—
said you need Dialectical Behavioral Therapy,
same as they told you last time
you went to the hospital three years ago.

And the pot we've been stirring begins to boil.

Maggie Running

Your dad and I are so happy
that you've gone back to running—

*Good sign that she's exercising—
stopped smoking—
cut down on her bar hopping.*

The latest boyfriend is a good influence.
He has a degree, a job, an apartment.
He runs.

For your 23rd birthday
we pile up the running presents—
Adidas shorts, knee-length pants,
a hot pink tank
and top-of-the-line gel ASICS,

and we have sunflowers at the party
and a dairy-free cake
for your allergy.

Surprise!

All for me? you say.

I should have known
when I saw
you were running
until your toes bled
you were going
too far
too fast.

The Therapy Room

The philodendron snakes
up the wall
and across the top
of the bare window,

hanging on gold hooks
carefully screwed
into the wood trim,

its quiet leaves
casting shadows
on white walls

as if another plant
grows behind the first,
only larger, darker—

a ghost of the real one.

You study the gnarled
plant as you sit in the office
each week,

a small, young woman
on a long, deep couch

with the philodendron creeping
beyond your psychologist
angling to find a way out.

Halloween

A holiday for ghouls
and princesses and fairies.

Each year you plan
your costume
and decorate
a parade of boyfriends
to win contests
at the local bars.

I watch you,
a winged Tinkerbell,
turn A.J. from a handsome,
blonde accountant
to a monster
with a bloody bolt protruding
from his forehead
for first prize.

Your last costume,
never worn and now
in a pink box on the shelf,
is a *Swan Lake* tutu.

October 15th,
with only six days more—
the package arrives.

I escape upstairs
annoyed that you're
ignoring your bills
and shopping online again

                                            (stanza break)

while you twirl in the garage
for your daddy,
white tulle and feathers flying
in the spooked October air.

To Maggie Wherever You've Gone

1.
After years of trying to grow sunflowers,
they popped up this summer
beyond the fence
in the field by the woods.
I had cast the seeds in late spring
almost casually, as a matter of routine,
expecting nothing,
but still hoping blindly.

They came with seeded faces,
burnt sienna orbs
surrounded by yellow flames—
starbursts in the morning
igniting the August air with golden innocence.

2.
When I try to sleep, I imagine
you in the chill basement
climbing on the wooden chair,
the one my sister bought me at a second-hand
store during my divorce,
the one I used when I painted the edges
along the ceilings while I looked for a new life.

I imagine you stepping up
holding your scarf,
jumping a little,
as I had done time and time again
balancing a bucket of paint,
your hand resting on the back

of the chair for leverage,
tying the double knot on the bar overhead,
estimating length
then tying another knot
beneath your fair hair
and around your slender neck.

The official certificate reads:
Cause of death: Asphyxia from neck compression.
Manner of death: Suicide.
Method of injury: Hanging.
Date: October 21, 2011.

The chair rode
to the dump the morning after
in the bed of your father's pickup,
rumbling down the driveway
with bottles and cans
and yesterday's news—
another piece of furniture discarded
with no one the wiser.

3.
A few days later
a storm drives across the back field
in the middle of the night--
a ghostly tractor reaping.
Wind from the northeast
rattles the panes we had shut
against the downpour.
In the morning,
the field is littered
with petals and hacked stems
jutting from the soaked earth,

twisted and broken like Halloween bones
scrambling away from the dawn.

Wind

When people die,
I tend to think of them going up
even though we dig
to place them under.

The first night after we find you,
when your father and I finally
dissolve into bed,
the wind blows circles
about the house,
whistling outside the window
like a boy
calling for his lost dog
in the dark.

I listen for a long time,
your father silent beside me.

Then I hear it,
barely,
a slender sort of singing
like a reed against pursed lips
fading into the abyss

and the hole
we began digging
grows deeper.

Memorial

Your mother spends the week
searching through the family photos
and modeling shoots,
choosing, organizing,
scanning the pictures into the computer.

The slideshow, set to music,
is the center of the memorial
where the front row is crowded
with old and current boyfriends crying

over elfish childhood grins,
soccer shots and Christmas mornings,
braces twinkling between thin lips,
and recent fashion poses
frozen by the photographer's lens.

Pictures of you are everywhere
like wallpaper—
on copper stands and in assorted frames
across the curtained tables,
staring next to bouquets
of sunflowers—
the entry and exits decorated
with your youth,
images and poses that did not breathe
smiling broadly from birth to twenty-three—

and in a lonely lavender and white urn,
shaped and fired by your mother's lover,
surrounded by a wreath of opalescent roses,
your ashes mutter,
waiting to be noticed.

Things You Left

Your lunch, packed for work, in the fridge.
Native American Dream Catcher.
Jewelry tree with spiny, black limbs, solitary necklace
    dangling.
Feathers from New England birds.
Earth-blue sushi plate snaked with ashes of incense.
Amber prescription bottles for Wellbutrin and Zoloft.
Expired aspirin.
Enemas.
Tall orange vase filled with scented flowers.
Salt rock night lamp.
Books on world religions and meditation.
Wuthering Heights and *The Age of Innocence*, novels
    I gave you.
False eyelashes and a rainbow of eye shadows.
Hats for all seasons.
The Bell Jar.
Watercolor paint and canvases.
Diaries, including the one recounting your previous
    attempt at 18 with the plastic bag.
Orange wingback chair in crushed velvet.
Atop the bookshelf: A card I wrote thanking you for
    helping at my birthday party
    featuring a picture of Heyerdahl's
    At the Window.
Dog-eared copy of *Lolita*.
Assorted lotions for day face, night face, elbows,
    hands, eyes, cuticles....
Green BMW, your 21st birthday present, cigarette
    burns curled through the tan leather
    along the driver's side window.
Laptop loaded with nude photos from dozens
    of modeling shoots.

Black and white picture of Marilyn, framed.
Cell phone with the record of your last outgoing calls
    to your boyfriend:
      11:12 pm, 11:13, 11:19.
Eight bags of clothes and shoes.
Seven bikinis and three beach towels.
One miniature conch shell at the bottom of a
    cosmetic organizer
      too delicate, too helpless for the sea.

Your Art

A huge bloody eye
in acrylics
that you labored over
and with which you were displeased.

A triptych of the back of you
nude
disjointed above your dresser.

Another nude of you, frontal pose,
centered,
surrounded by the large profile
of a dark-haired man with a beard in one corner
and a small child in the opposite corner
curled up in a ball.

Silhouettes of trees
and two lovers
face to face against
a passionate sunset sky.

The lists you made
on poster board
I didn't see until after—
reasons to live on one side,
reasons to die on the other.

And hidden behind the Marilyn Monroe photo—
a watercolor:
multiples of you at the bottom of
the ocean rising
out of a seaweed jungle.

Loud

I once listened to a man
bellowing in a field
by the Moose Mill River
with the cold wind pressed against him—

his pregnant wife gone only a few days,
someone he had waited until mid-life to meet,
mowed down at the mailbox
by a speeding adolescent.

What he got in return
was winter slapped across his face.

I cannot breathe for sorrow and cannot control my
own sobbing—

dearest Maggie,

hanging hidden in a basement
when the noose
you wore to dinner
Pass the peas, please
was tightening every evening
in plain sight.

Blame

Your suicide
is a necklace
of strung beads

of mother, father,
brother,
grandparents,
aunts, uncles,
lovers, friends

worn tight against your neck.

When broken,
each tiny sphere
bounced
to its own corner,

pinholes like
accusing eyes
glaring
at one another.

The Break-Up

I don't see it coming
but I should have.
It was barreling toward us
like a train at high speed,
wailing grief.

When your dad moves out,
he's a fist poised to throw
a knock-out punch.
I don't duck.

Three weeks later I find the
inscription on the beam
above the wooden clothes rod that held you—

Maggie Mason 6/25/1988-10/21/2011
Always and forever, sweet girl
Love you, Dad.

I paint over it before a realtor
comes to assess the house.
He says I don't have
to reveal the truth unless
I'm directly asked.
The beam was an advertisement.

I stay because
moving is too expensive,
but pulling your long hairs from the drain,
listening for your footsteps
on the basement stairs,

living alone with the fear
that whatever dark wave took you
is welling within me, too,
proves to be far more costly.

The Weight of You

That morning as I searched for you
I heard creaking, almost like a moan,
in the basement.

I called your name, and called again.
You were on the other side of the wall,
a dangling pocket watch,
face frozen,
lips parted as though asking for air.

After I cut you down,
I realized what I'd heard
was the tension on the rod.
When your dad took it to the dump,
he said he was surprised it didn't break
under your weight.

Now eight months later,
by Providence
or accident of bald coincidence,
I land in the same office
with the philodendron
snaking around the window.
The psychologist I'm referred to
shares space with your doctor
on alternate evenings.
What are the chances?

I sit on the same big couch
and gaze at the same outrageous
vine of tangled leaves
and desperate stems clawing at the window

looking for a way out.

Tonight, my psychologist
tells me I'm overidentified with you,
gives me his cell phone number,
just in case—

the weight of you is pendulous,
still straining all around.

Unraveling

It is said that in every
suicide, there are
at least six people
who are left at risk.

You made the choice
for exit seem so
easy—

only thirty seconds
before sleep.

Have you found distance
in white light
from what I
alone here
now face?

You have thrown
me back into
myself,
unraveled the stitches
of my own wounds
oozing grief as black
as the narrow hallways
into history.

Damn the scarf
that took you,
the madness
in your spirit,

(stanza break)

this lonely keyboard,
banging out words
like bullets.

In the midst of heartache—

a procession of fragrant
spring mornings
pinned together
like white cotton sheets
on the clothesline.

Poem for Your 24th Birthday

There is the opposite
of celebration
without you.

I ask your dad
if he wants to take
a walk with me,
but he prefers
to be alone.

Later a friend
told me she saw
him in her headlights
running full speed
down the center
of Rte. 88 that night

but couldn't see
what chased him.

First Anniversary 2012

I buy a stone bench
and place it in the back field,
mow a path
and a circle around it—

plant three flowering saplings—
two dogwoods pink and red,
a pear tree with white blossoms—
off the deck in the backyard
imagining limbs spread
like dancers' arms
and fruit hanging like jewelry.

I call your grandmothers, father, brother
on their cell phones
and leave meandering messages.

I sit in noon sun
eating yogurt
on the bench you'll never see
watching bees dance
on the last wildflowers
of summer.

That night,
the city wet with a post-supper shower,
my voice trembles as I read
To Maggie Wherever You've Gone
in a Bedford church,
its cavernous room
bare of breathing
like the gaping mouth of a tomb.

The Letter

I write to your psychologist
because I keep thinking about her
when I visit the philodendron.

Her business cards and coffee mug
stare at me across the room
as I ramble on to my own therapist
from the long couch
about sleepless nights and your ash gray image.
In a long letter, I tell her in detail
what happened after you left her office
on that last autumn afternoon.

Dear Doctor,
You don't know me. I was Maggie's father's
partner...

I imagine her shock
when she heard what you'd done.
How many times she must have
replayed that last session in her mind.
What did I miss? Should I have guessed?

I tell her you lied about taking your medication.
I also bet she didn't know
your esophagus was burned from excessive vomit—
and about your mounting debt, and too many men,
the steady diet of risks you thrived on—
how you waved suicide like a flag
in front of those of us who loved you—
that you'd left a will and instructions
for your funeral in the middle of a spiral notebook.

(stanza break)

She is grateful for the letter,
though the words fell off the page
and hit the floor screaming
because no one can treat a lie.

Nude Model

You told me
you kept your clothes on

except just once
for art—

but your laptop
tells a different story.

Hundreds of photos, Maggie,

no clothes,
not a stitch

in hundreds of
changing backdrops,

maybe borderline artistic.

And then one man
with a camera raped you

and you wised up
and quit the business.

For what it's worth,
it wasn't art that failed you.

One Thousand Emails

It's the harshest winter in a century.
Snow swells the rooftops
to three times their size
and ice dams flow over the eaves
like rivers frozen in mid-air.
For a month, I have to park
at the bottom of the long driveway
and trudge up the hill to the house in heavy boots.
Bereft and lonely on a Friday night,
television yacking like an old woman in curlers
at the beauty parlor,
I hear a commercial for *match.com*.

He is too old for me,
but his profile says he used to be a priest.
I go right for the jugular.
Is there a God in heaven...Then how could He?

My online priest takes a long breath and speaks to me
out of the deep well of himself,
from dark waters,
a rising bucket
until I can see my own reflection.

He has been widowed for 25 years
and knows the tumult of a turbulent childhood,
young love lost, a career in shambles—
has both cursed God and begged
for mercy prostrate on the stone floor
of an Episcopal sanctuary,
with two young children to raise by himself
on the paltry salary of a parish priest.

(stanza break)

One thousand emails back and forth
full of why and how and if only,
whittling the second winter away,
you gone and me still reeling,
wrapped in a woolen blanket,
typing my sins to a stranger.

Poem for Your 25th Birthday

Still the opposite of celebration,
I make an ass of myself
by downing shots of whiskey
and scaling Miller's Hill
where your father spread your ashes.

I sprinkle pink rose petals
from my own birthday bouquet
along the path in the rain
at two a.m.

The next morning,
bleary-eyed and in full headache,
I go back to see what
I'd done in the dark.

The side of the hill
is in blossom with wildflowers
of every color.
I pick small petals
from their bones
and throw them like confetti
over the fallen roses.

One week later,
I see no trace of my passing there,
as if the earth
had swallowed my folly,
entombed my grief.

Ashes to Ashes

I scale the hill again today
where your ashes are—
where rain has swept the summer heat
under a carpet of low clouds,
leaving puddles in the long grass.
I watch the sky reaching
with its fog fingers
into the treetops
and see ghosts descending.

How could you I still wonder
as my socks and pants soak through.

Your ashes—
have they traveled to a playground
on a child's rubber sole,
become the grass
and nimbus?

I find you nowhere and everywhere
on this hilltop,
and in these words
and the spaces between the words
as I hurry away
to hoard my own dust.

Scarf

The image rises when
I least expect it.

You dangling
by that cotton scarf
bought on a shopping spree.

Sheer, with pink and white stripes—

a shawl
for your neck and shoulders
in summer.

A frame for your oval face
and blue eyes.

How happily
you must have tossed
it around yourself
in the mirror
after snipping off the tag

racing about
high on retail joy
from something
that still smelled like store

bouncing out the door to get in the car,
scarf tail flapping out the open window
as you sped down the gravel driveway,

you and your fabric rope
plotting an execution.

How Many Times More—

Funny how I notice
red hair and ponytails
on young women running,
driving fast in their cars,
reading the ingredients
on the side of the box
in the cereal aisle.

They could be you
still moving through your life.

Sometimes my eyes linger too long
looking for resemblance,
then turn away.

How many times more—
there and gone again?

Grief

Curled up in a ball
on the unmade bed
in late morning

quilted by a patch of sun,

my mind hanging in half-sleep
like wind-blown laundry—

those many men you spread your thighs for—
the drugs, the lies and daily vomit swirling in a
flush—
what is it you accomplished?

We all dig holes we can't climb out of,

or bury ourselves in too much asking.

Hemlock

What curtain falls
what manner of emptiness
what prickly pang of loneliness
leads to the final surrender?

Maggie,
your end remains both
a bloated mystery
and a dram of hemlock
swirling in a cup.

Perhaps each of us
in our own dark hour
must tremble on the cliff,
the window ledge—
feel the noose
tied taut against the neck
while teetering on a wooden chair—
to be absolutely sure that we
would never jump.

Bouquet

Every time I think I'm through,
grief calls to me again.

It's a door that opens
to a spirit singing,

then closes

on silence.

Are you to become a void—
someone unremembered

as if you were a bouquet
of summer wildflowers gone by?

Life travels on
and I go with it—

somehow I must carry you,
brown petals falling.

Second Anniversary 2013

I have this thing
about you and sunflowers.

I don't even know if you liked them.

Two years ago, I sowed sunflower seeds
that blossomed before a storm hit
a few days after we lost you.

I see a giant sunflower balloon
bobbing in the flower shop
above splendid pink gladiolas.
I buy it to tie to your bench
in the back field
on the second anniversary.

I wonder if you can see a balloon,
if you can see anything.

A sunflower balloon is probably a dumb idea
in the winds of New England autumn,
but I'll anchor it,
watch it weave and bob,
do everything I can to keep it,
against the odds.

Microburst II

You can hardly see
the fallen trees five years later.
Vines have bundled them up
and hidden the upheaval.
New branches shoot out
of trees that lean, but still live.

On a July morning,
I pause along the path hikers
have forged around the rubble
a dog at my heels.

The forest buzzes with renewal.

Acknowledgements

The Awakenings Review, 2020,
    "Scarf"
    "To Maggie Wherever You've Gone"
    "Ashes to Ashes"
    "Bouquet"
    "The Therapy Room"

Gramercy Review, 2024,
    "Photographer's Model"

I am grateful to the publications where some of these poems appeared, sometimes in slightly different form.

About the Author

Photo by Sue Lipsky

Christine Andersen is a retired dyslexia specialist who hikes every day in the Connecticut woods with her five hounds, pen and pad in pocket. She holds a BA in Creative Writing and an MA in Counseling Psychology. A decade ago, she founded a fund at the University of Connecticut to enhance training in trauma for future psychologists with the hope of putting more trauma-informed professionals in the field. She has published over 100 poems, won the 2023 American Writers Review Poetry Contest, and in 2024, the Lee Mae's Memorial Award #1 in the National Poetry Day Contest of Massachusetts, and the Choeofpleirn Press Harvest Harmonies 2024 Contest. This is her first chapbook.

Judge's Comments

To Maggie Wherever You've Gone is a chapbook-length elegy to a young woman who committed suicide by hanging herself. While these poems contain specific details, the poems often end with resonant images and metaphors, allowing the "words [to]...hit the floor screaming" before the poet, in visiting the hill where this woman's ashes were scattered, believes that "the earth/ had swallowed my folly,/ entombed my grief." These poems move from grief to bewilderment before repeating these steps. Ultimately, the poet reaches a kind of recognition in that the desire to kill ourselves may sometimes exist, and it takes "feel[ing] the noose / tied taut against the neck...to be absolutely sure that we / would never jump."

Choeofpleirn Press' poetry editor, James P. Cooper, author of *Listening for Low Tide*, judged this contest.

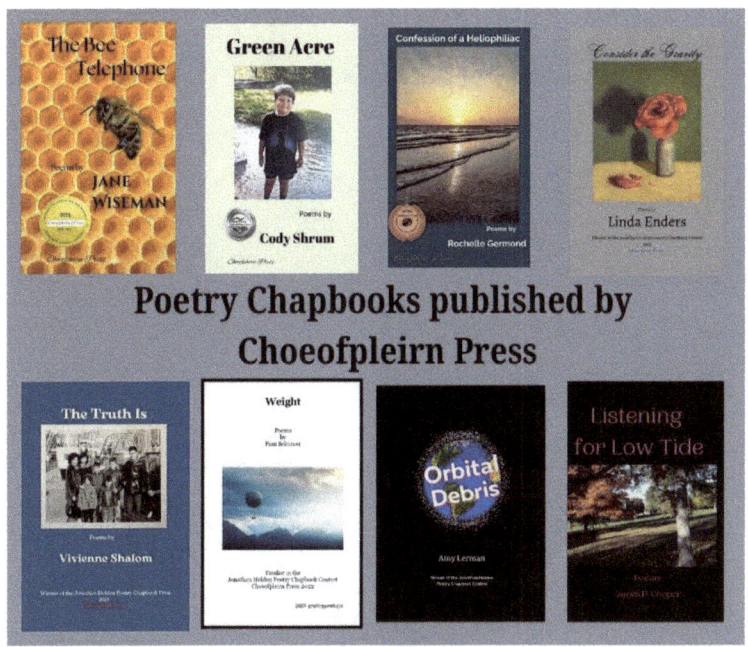

See our other titles at our Bookstore.

Choeofpleirn Press

2025

A product of the state of Kansas
www.choeofpleirnpress.com

www.ingramcontent.com/pod-product-compliance
Lightning Source LLC
Chambersburg PA
CBHW060537030426
42337CB00021B/4314